The Moon's Reminder

Kevin Gillam

The Moon's Reminder

Acknowledgements

Some of these poems have been published in the following journals:
Meanjin, Southerly, Westerly, Overland, Australian Poetry Journal, Unusual Work, Page Seventeen, Australian Love Poems Anthology, Poetry D'Amour Anthology (2012/13/14), *Writ Poetry Review, Axon, Famous Reporter, Cullens Wine Poetry Collection, Writing to the Edge Anthology, Sawtooth ARI Review, Tamba, The Mozzie, Award Winning Australian Writing, Sitelines, Leaf Press, Cordite, Eureka Street, Creatrix, Blue Giraffe, Sotto* and *Dot-Dot-dash*

Some poems have also been awarded prizes:
'a kind of swimming': 1st Prize Patrons Poetry Prize PCWC 2013
'the moon's reminder': 1st Prize Sawtooth ARI Writing Awards 2015
'the hush': Highly Commended Page Seventeen Awards 2012
'chamber musing': Highly Commended Glen Phillips Poetry Prize 2014
'the stroking': 1st Prize Manly FAW Awards 2011
'softer dark': 1st Prize Katharine Susannah Prichard
Writing Awards 2012
'seven dreams round': 1st Prize Katharine Susannah Prichard
Writing Awards 2015
'napkin man': 1st Prize Inter Stellar Poetry Awards 2015
'the colour of healing': 1st Prize Mental Health Week Competition 2016
'and still': 1st Prize OOTA Spilt Ink Competition 2016

The Moon's Reminder
ISBN 978 1 76041 537 2
Copyright © text Kevin Gillam 2018
Cover image: *Tide Travellers*, Edna Broad

First published 2018 by
GINNINDERRA PRESS
PO Box 3461 Port Adelaide 5015
www.ginninderrapress.com.au

Contents

Mothers (and others)	9
silents	11
another sea	12
love	13
in the end	14
(not enough words for those to be tongued)	15
unmourning	17
those sweet things	18
the depth of a day	19
the day you came	21
the anaesthetist's share	22
switch and none	24
sugar into butter	25
'stay'	26
song of other	27
orders	28
silvering to blue	29
slack-jawed in the dark	31
softer dark	34
figue	36
death rattle	37
better without cloud	38
'73	39
Airfix hours	40
Maps	43
the tides	45
stone to sky	46
porch	47
in the lane where I live	48

in the street	49
toffee ap	50
there and not	51
the road	52
the map breathers	53
something unclocked	54
seven dreams round	55
scent through	57
more than half a sonnet	58
Nannup Diary	59
Kulin	60
hieroglyphics of now?	61
(every colour makes yellow)	62
enough notes for disappointment	63
contrapunctus a 4	64
all the thoughts	66
a kind of swimming	67
equal lengths	69
Masks	**71**
the soup of us	73
unclearing	74
Thurs	75
these bleak days	76
the stolen one	77
the hush	78
thanxxs for contributing	79
is it?	80
the purpling	81
the point?	83
the one of us	88
the hours	89
the groove of you	90

the colour of healing	91
the boys	92
out here	93
napkin man	94
me?	97
lingers	98
east block	99
display pome	100
darks	101
chamber musing	102
bent truth and belief	105
and leave	107

Moths — 109

the line that failed me	111
punctuated sky	112
louvred light	113
learnts	114
in my absence	115
hopes	116
still as moss	117
sonnet breathing	118
silence isn't yellow	119
moth words	120
propped	122
a crooked eye	124
and the wind	125
drinking why	126

Moons — 127

the less heard	129
Venus	130
unknown skies	131

two notes	132
the weight of angst?	133
the same moon	134
the night for knots	135
the moon's reminder	136
seven sutures	137
old stones	138
the sound of black	139
last bits	140
his walk, not mine	141
fiction is necessary	142
but they say	143

Mothers (and others)

silents

'i' hasn't slipped out of 'silents' – not yet –
can't not hear what can be heard –

yet, with your eyes plucked shut
you won't buy less or more than

what's implied – walls around oils,
a type of unbruising that won't be

sliced out. that's her, sitting next to you,
sutures for lips, perfume of brine

off an incoming tide. but she's
jettyless, no slap or slide, and

nil and ice leave but a fleece
inside her. like an imaginary

cat on polished boards. 'marpa's the
word for it, the 'i' slipped between

another sea

had a friend called epiphany
always asking, 'do you love me?'
my answer, 'maybe'
never satisfactory
of course, she
searching for lock and key,
my desire for other fish, another sea

love

goes fishing. off a bridge.
catches one. big.
into the bucket. threshing.
and flicking. eyes unblinking.
beckoning. come with me.
back to the river. and love.
forgets why it came. and jumps

in the end

in the end, when he went it was
so quick. in the end he was seated
in kitchen chair, as if

writing a letter, as if listening
to the wireless, as if thinking.
in the end he was in

sandals and white singlet with
slicked back white hair, mouth slightly

ajar as if beginning to speak.
in the end it was the shell
of him, the carapace,

the very empty box of him.
in the end he wasn't there,
me ready to tell him I was

(not enough words for those to be tongued)

so you're better tonight
but
read better as bandaged

and you've had instincts of
nine,
two bars plus fermata,

but as you ascend the
bricked
serendipity of

the blind you begin to
fear
what the morrow might bring.

so see it as a jour-
ney
down the fingerboard of

cello, from middle C
to
aural stratosphere, hear

it as the primaeval
wash
of chords i to vi, you

as flotsam, tossed, pike fish,
one
eye away from weed. for

now, collapse into this
temp-
orary place of ease.

what hovers? velour wait-
ing
room, lino moment. door

begins, he opens. in-
breath,
'your scans, yes, they've come back'

unmourning

propped. on the couch. with your foot. rubbing
and leaving. on the couch. with my book.
robbing and propped. on the out. on

the take. with a ticket. with your foot.
propped. the book symphonic. this flimsy

now. your foot. propped. but whose fabric?
whose dance? words and dermis. proofed.
propped. your book. the foot. in no mood. the

book. with your foot. call it sleeving.
paragraphs of skin. tactile reading.
rounded. pronounced. propped. your foot. hymn to

now. the book. vespering. drawing in
wet air. forgetting. propped. on the couch.
book and foot. unmourning. practising now

those sweet things

and I'm up to put an end to night and make
a start to day and you say with your mouth
full of oats that you've found a rhyme for the
fruit with peel and pith and pips and you say this
with an oat on your lip and you say its those

sweet things you suck when you've got a cold but I
say I don't know what you mean and then you

get peeved and sulk and say you'll take your words
and hide them and not let me play and I say
how 'bout a rhyme for the hue that's more dark than
mauve and that makes you stop the chew and muse and

this is our start of day and this is the start
to all our days and its weird how we find
rhymes for fruit and hues but can't find rhyme in us

the depth of a day

she sits, in her plenty,
in her squalor. behind her
the dog wheezes in sleep,
bar heater ticks arthritic.
behind her rests another
vacant day, a cloudless sky
when keening for rain.
she's thinking about that,
about what's behind, in front

In Remembrance
Timothy Arthur Boyd

do we move through hours
or stand still as hours glide
around us? who snips the
deadheads of spent time?

1981–2005
To my hazel-eyed one

clasping her hands, she notices
the blueness of veins snaking
across bone. why blue
and not red? she thinks

War took you young.
God keeps you close.

from beyond the window a
car door slams, a car starts.
life's about that. closing
and going. she remembers
thinking that before

Mum

'life's about making knots in
the frayed but same coloured ends.'
she says this out loud, nodding
to herself, nodding to the
uniformed young face in the frame,
knowing that she's felt
the depth of a day

the day you came

it was good, and if I'd read my stars
that day I would have found it was
bound to be, would have joined the dots of
fate, the day you slipped through the sky and came
to me. there you stood, glint off sea no
match for your wrap of blue and sheen, charms
strung tight as beads, looped through chat, you so
keen to talk of wings and drift, warm air
that might bid you, yes, on this, the day

you came. me? I was snared, bit, stung, blessed,
floored, found – all of these. and clouds went from
scrawl to sense, leaves danced and blushed then
drew their breath, the moon spun and showed its
not seen side, the day you came to me

the anaesthetist's share

am breathing in sunshine, in silence,
in an afternoon still as regret.

you're not with me, off and not,
on the tongue, all that's unsaid.

we are vespers. we are all sung.
we have been out here, bushfired sunsets,

cinders of betweens. and there is you,
ghost limb, collection bowl, a throb,

a guilt, a staining, as if am
moth-winged fingered, as if have been

mouthing hymns, forgetting, like
losing north, surrendering

the anaesthetist's share. but
am breathing out pasts and make-believe

to this smashed up sky, to the
twigs on doorsill, am setting traps.

but, turning left, moving right,
with the hum of wires, this seagull heart,

words long as notes, not yet
at the crossing of leaving/longing,

in the could of did. this smeltered now,
blood and time and water,

or, perhaps, the weight of silence,
bar lines through hours unplayed.

perhaps bark has ceased book ending.
where are the small deities

for frail thinking, the lakes for intincting?
where sits the drum of scalded leaves,

your gun-powered maps and creeds?

switch and none

you're in. can't get. and none. in
that room. switch and none. out and

I. on a string. get out and.
of forty watts. none window

and. room of forty watts. you
can't get out. and none window.

on a string. and none switch. can't
get out. that room. forty watts

on. you're in. you can't. I can't.
and none. can't get. window and.

can't get. none switch and. and I
can't. you can't. I can't get in

sugar into butter

won't be a shagpiled sky,
be high up smeared cirrus
as you breathe it in.
'goodness', 'nurture', 'flourish' –
mother as you hear her all ways,
the sun-warped tape of days
scented with camellias, sifted fine
or rubbed, sugar into butter.

feel a clammy forgotten
of days lemon-edged, sepia-hued,
the fingernail flicked lips to teeth,
stolen from that sister – rapture –
entrapped, then cast upward,
one sliver at a time

'stay'

the in-breath,
suck of air across
lips and tongue and teeth –
kept from the
first take –
'green light',
voice husky,
'seven eleven',
shagpiling down
into minor ii,
pulling me back
to Heathrow,
departures,
last hug

song of other

asleep you are lithe
curled between weed and floater,
a song of other

I stoop, hold and let
your whispers find stone, find tide,
asleep you are so lithe

then unravelling
gift of whiteness undefined,
one song of other

cadence of gather
and exhalation, waves' rush,
asleep you and lithe

turned on memory's
wheel as the spume chases day,
lost song of other

now trapped in forget,
a dust from moon's ne'er seen side,
asleep you are lithe,
a song of other

orders

there is, was, could be, should be an order
to your dying but there will, won't be

nurses and order-
lies silent as ladybirds, humming like bees

needle into crêpe-paper veins – orders
but not yours

in those last hours, an order-
ly flight of birds across a yellowing page

morning billowing into afternoon – the order
unmasked – into night

it's the look, drip down, logic, order
of truths on stone

can see the black in the blue, orders
from the god of betweens

silvering to blue

i

'first mouthed, last swallowed' your favourite line,
'avoid what is to come', papering lips,

uttered. favourite lines your compulsion,
ready as quills, papered lips uttering,

all rasp and spittle. compulsions, ready
as quills, silent but waiting, just rasp

and spittle. 'avoid what is to come', the
weight of silence? 'first mouthed, last swallowed'

ii

have this photograph. you.
standing, with axe. folklore

in that. on the quarter-
acre. white singlet. fine

sinewy muscles of
legs. beside the chopped tuart.

clear day. sunlight, haloed,
you, smiling. hair brilled, slick.

no need for words. axe and
saw having spoken

iii

there's none more rush, at mind's
guitar now, none more hurry. you've

that bright wet smile, propped on
plastic sea, none more rush. north long

forgotten, just fluorescence,
none more hurry. nurses have

come, taken blood, stories –
there's none more rush. skin and

yearnings silvering to blue,
none more hurry. shush of

undriving, rim of things, strumming,
none more rush, none more hurry

slack-jawed in the dark

Wagin 1944

after the unsilence, my father walks,
walks out the bruise and fret of the school yard
long crept inside him. from behind, his

wounded form, the stronger and bullied,
both breathing. a flock of sulphur-cresteds,
like torn pages in wind, watches, wheels

overhead. a salt lake on town's edge,
waiting, froths at its rim. late afternoon,
my father dawdling, his shadow owning

him, monday, piano lesson looming.
and above it all, wind through the
leaves of salmon gums, like sandpaper

on the bricks in the old silo, my father,
walking, a cappella for one

Perth 1953

polyphony draws him, my father,
draws him to the city, entwines him,
infuses him like incense. in the
sanctum of the choir loft, amongst prayer

cushions and candelabras, the soft and
polished and flickering, he finds other
gravities, pares away the flare and bleed
of hours past. my father hears a new

language – '*melisma*', '*tierce da picardi*' –
rubs a finger across ritual
and smoothed pew. but it's the psalm and creed,
the right hand cupped in left, the forsaken,

humble, not so worthy, communion
of flesh and thought that sings to my father

Albany 2011

slack jawed in the dark he plays it out,
my father, Irving Berlin's 'When I'm

Calling You', all the blacks, memory's
spume, his boyhood dance hall hands still vamping,

not knowing how. music is the salve,
circling and rubbing, sewing was to is.

beyond the veranda, the sound under
cirrus, matt finished. just two jetty stumps

left – serial number of National
Service rifle and the name of his wife –

a duet, that, and the pianola
rolls of songs that live in my father's hands,

after the salt has risen, after a
new word, 'fermata', before the silence

softer dark

and you are seated, in singlet, at laminex table, the box tree
crickling out its name, light fluorescent,

leaves 'neath a shagpile sky, and it's a kind of unthinking this,
you loosely skinned, not still,

won't be still. light gone to milk, the table sheathed,
clouds loosely arranged, letters, soft focus

the wrong word for it. déjà vu hides day,
your cold forehead the script, of course, all this rapid and fragile

and washed under, were you washed under? they've come,
taken limbs, had to, more torso than bark,

all in order. the dead frisk us –
was trying to sing that, for a waxing gibbous moon,

light like cellophane, you seated, slinked open,
empty. these bees, these scrawlings. you are ringed, unsapped,

being stilled, stilling. grieve harbours eve and ever watchful,
but wary. shines, the table, yes, pages,

cross-hatched cirrus, and you decades high. you went, weren't then,
walls aching with news, moth-winged light, clock stopped

and bark ticking, dust motes and anthem hanging, tree
rhyming in green. the verge raked and raw, medals next

to cloud, scent of forget. polyphony –
bark beneath palm, fur and glass, no longer reacting

to the light. when it rains, pages unbrailled, and I've
come to you, skin, a breeze shuffling Sound.

kitchen table, and its surface, gleaming sky.
then you, forehead clammy, blowfly humming at screen door,

you seated, light gone to pixels, you sifted
and raked and stacked, and you still,

you're stilling. your verge hours, brittling now, waiting,
cheekbones in sunlight, seamless, way they

removed the limbs. you upright, seated, 4 p.m., light louvred,
you stilled, being stiller. you more bark, more shabby

than torso, when it comes time to die, sky unkempt,
unedged, and bees in the rain? you were seated, in singlet

and they'll come to you, your cold forehead and not
that I kissed, they'll come, in softer dark

and fold your limbs, came. this, and being still, be stilled, still

figue

*my father's favourite fruit was a fig
and, like a fig,
my father flowered on the inside*

Wagin, 1947, salt lakes and Salmon Gums,
post-war frugality, dance hall, my father the
vamping pianist, railway town, Baptist tracks rattling

*fig, from the French 'figue',
a soft pear-shaped, many-seeded fruit*

clattering atop keys, my father's hands, all the blacks,
not knowing how, the band,
paid in riders, post-gig drinks

*dun brown the fig or a bruised purple,
call it petulant, or shy*

sly kinship, the held look, man lingers
over man, my father, call it ekphrastic,
phrases hungering for another's art

*fruiting twice each season, 'breva',
the first crop, on woody stems*

my father, Baptist tracks clattering

flowering on the inside

death rattle

'the death rattle' – Tex's phrase for salt shaker,
driving home, Dragon's 'Are You Old Enough' on

Jurassic FM, soft focus and over the Swan,
Tex propped home, off his scooter at the lights and

spare tones of violins, low rotation but no, this
Port city doesn't need buildings 'cos its got boats

and Marc Hunter is dead and not page before
thought as river bleeds to sea, faux wrench of chorus,

in Tex's Homeswest unit scent of Vix and wet flannel,
metal on metal from the Freo line and

Jesus was a prisoner, yes? limestoned in by morals,
a cold and lonely lyric that, and where's God in all

of this, where are you God? Tex swathed in tracksuit
and ABC, soluble moon, 'cos you were a boxer Tex,

a mid-ship man, masseuse, guitar player, drummer,
down South Street hum of trucks, whiff of sheep, now in

your Jason Recliner Rocker wheezing out a day, neons
of Hampden stay on, neap tide, chorus, but could that

be you Tex? fluoro on the blink? once so bright behind
the kit? Rottnest winks, waning gibbous moon talcs a

verse, the hip Tex, the spine, the mind, stone ghosts of
Asylum, sea seeps disguised as river, as

a line lies dropped in a lane, moon sits cryptic, trains and Macs
and snare and is that you Tex, your death rattle?

better without cloud

if you pen sun and love first,
lasts slide from memory,
the link of course, the lyric of warm

we met, in colder climes,
on a beach called Exhaustion,
a high school metaphor 'rockmelon rind'
Alpine cigarette commercial ('Fresh is the flavour') arc,
sand white as absence

we met, a gnarled and frayed piece of
orange rope, half a conch shell (architecture
of idea?), flotsam, de-found

beach regained breath. right now,
be nice to hear some rain on our tin roof.
back then, we were better without cloud

'73

they're off to a
progressive dinner,
mother in crocheted poncho,
father in safari suit,
complete with dish of apricot chicken,
box of splades and
bottle of Ben Ean moselle.

me?
I'm at home in my
flares watching
H.R. Pufnstuf –
the economic
rationalists are yet
to be born

Airfix hours

you arrive on time, usual, while
I've just finished slicing sunshine and

putting it into Tupperware, usual,
and the day, given it's pre-dawn shape of

question mark, usual, but without point,
usual, sits in the shade of angst and

we tune you to me, usual, because one
of yours keeps slipping badly, usual,

and there's a moon and ragdoll cat and
some late Haydn, and, towards the end, talk

of the sea, all quite usual, but then
the day unbends, what was closing and

inflecting straightens and opens, most
unusual, because, in the last of

our guidings towards harmonics, and just
how to put this, usual, it comes to

me that the idea of something, the
visual imagining, my being

ambushed by a memory from the
future, rather than those authentic

Airfix hours of box opening,
following instructions, gluing, being

and doing, this is where gravity
drags and drowns me, highly usual,

yes, and the point, the day's point,
unusual, is how my next gnaws at now

Maps

the tides

you would say that it was tidal,
all to do with the tides.
yes, you would say that
and I would look away, look west

we're doing things in halves today,
you would say that,
a day in halves,
only was there ever a day that was whole?

have you finished writing about tomorrow?
you said that.
no I said, haven't finished with the yesterdays

I'm driving now, driving and thinking,
away, and thriving.
I could say that, could say that

stone to sky

on the surface. wings fan-
ning. minuscule ripples.
bee in circles. light spang-
ling. the surface. soundless.
frantic, looping. palm spooned
beneath. wings. and bee. cupped.
rising. harbouring. loops.

the bee. tea spooned. wings on
skin. letting. legs scrambling.
drips. palm emptying. walk-
ing now. legs feathering.
ferried. the bee. edge. skin
to stone. legs and wings. blur-
ring. bee. lifts. stone to sky

porch

porch
close of day
scraps for migraine

porched
letter box
slit and slatered

porching
(verb)
umbral between doors

deporched
(behaviour)
not there

porchless
maps of clay

in the lane where I live

in the lane where I live it slopes down, slopes South, to the West the
poached egg of sun, and the lane has no lights, no kerbs, no paths but

has wild herbs, four types of rose and daubs of weed and the walls in
the lane are made of stone, of brick and the one three up from us,

of wood, has been clipped and chopped and bashed and propped and in this lane
the folk don't work, well not much, 'cept us and the one down from us

has two floors with lots of frills, all for two old folk with loads in
the bank but far less in their days but they do speak to us, in

their patched up, pranged up tongue and the house at the end has no plants –
no pots, no shrubs, no trees back or front while we live in a lush

plot of seeds and greens and blooms and dreams and we try to make sweet
noise, try to make each a nice day, try to make a note to thumb

tack to our fore heads which says 'we're here, we're new and we'd like to
like you', but I don't think the folk in the lane like blood or rhyme

in the street

in the
street where
I live
there are
these fine
people,
clear-eyed,
upright,
these mem-
ories,
doused in
petrol,
dancing,
flaming

toffee ap

Sunday split
ting, that ache
between prom
ise and rut,
post elect
ion, red bunt
ing bedrag

gled, talk of
core and bleed
ing, like side
show alley,
Royal Show,
toffee ap
ples in rain

there and not

upside down in the dark,
all the consonants, the
bent vowels, the syllables

dancing. losing north, gid-
dy in sunshine, all the
commas and hyphens, the

in-breaths, moist betweens fall-
ing. propped, not smoothed, beneath
a fugue of clouds, all the

smeared voices, extrava-
gant uses of steam. late
afternoon, light like strained

tea, all the truths, like mu-
sic in wind, there and not

the road

the road scars right, across the
palm of land, tumbling, dwindling,
a groove, a history, a way in,
worn and healed slick

the road, oil on linen, bitumen
on peat, with all its gradations
of shadow, bruise to smear to brush

the road, cloud above scuffed and
tugged by wind, rain sifting down,
the 'haar' they call it here,
cold breath of wet

the road, its dip and sway, blur
of scrub, the urge, glimpse of roof,
swerve, the early dark, the entrance

the map breathers

at dawn, sea is breathing, the pylons like staves unplayed,
feeling the easterlies, loose in their tethers while around the perimeter

bruising cloud, on the rocks one gull, cries scraping and insistent,
holding this tarpaulin, this vast lung of tepid thinks and

humidity, this salt and flung fish inhalation, but no need
to ponder – let the Sound lick, let history and now be

judged by the swelling in your scabbed shins, the same lengths
bitten and held by memory, one each of pith and kindling,

aches long slipped into incandescence while here, beneath
soles, the neaping, the fret, the conch and its unfurling,

architecture at its most naïve, here the tossed in calcified light,
dunes and scree and scuff into aquamarine, granite

tackling the tide, bookending glitter, the crêped and silvered
before Michaelmas and Breaksea, but this proximous thumb

nail, don't see it as Mistaken, no, one digit's armour,
angles of import, no, see it as sanctuary and the way a land

might kerchief its weepings, like hope might candle wax for more,
be forever drip, the channel 'tween the known and whimper of

prayer running neck deep against the schemers, the land borne,
the map breathers, those that front bar and banter and plot,

the shufflers, moving their plunder, all navigation and
nulling of surf and boulder, blind to scrub and pike fish,

lost as story, as bottle dropped, as gulled, as dawn

something unclocked

cut and swathed by salt and fret –
run your hands across this place
and something unclocked

feel it's stubbly truth,
get blisters from history,
cut and swathed by salt and fret

pool table smooth in parts,
then scraggly as grandma's chin
and something unclocked

a sort of relief map
and yes, palms bleeding,
swathed and cut by salt and fret

but this land won't know,
won't remember your touch
or the unclocked

will furl back the way it came,
slink back to its shagpile
and something unclocked,
cut and swathed by salt and fret

seven dreams round

out, one mile out off Goode Beach,
the 'Whales' Graveyard', surface scuffed
and tugged but three fathoms down
and seven dreams round, a cairn
of bones, tide combing at fronds
of seagrass, the handwriting

of the dropped, shunned by writings
of time, cartilage on beach
shy reminders beside fronds
and pike fish and flotsam scuffed
by Southerlies, ashened cairn
shedding its story all down

the shoreline, songs of whale down
in the dance of tide writing,
in Phrygian mode, a cairn's
history, blood from Cheynes Beach
Whaling Station purpling scuffed
seas, shark fins crazing, the fronds

out and and below in wait, fronds
thriving on gristle. and down
now in this hushed grove, scuffing
breeze atop, what is written?
what is remembered? a beach
of whalebone whispers, a cairn

calcium-rich, lush, a cairn
home to exotic fish, fronds
and flora unseen and beach
white as forget, the sky down
and matt finishing, writing
briny fiction on waves, scuffed

but holding, greedy sea, scuffed,
bones stolen, hunkered in cairn,
the orb of sunlight writing
in kelp and weed and green fronds,
wrasse and black brim darting down
and through undergrowth, Goode Beach

cradling and keeping its fronds
and flensed tales, while out, a cairn,
one mile out, watches a beach

scent through

red painted path. geraniums and
caterpillars. moist earth. rubber mat.
thumb, doorbell. hallway. wet dog.
forgiving berber. lounge. lemon cake.
tapestries. china cabinet. best
never used. dining table. doilies.
shortbread. rattle of hanging beads.

kitchen. corned silverside. yellow
bench tops. split lips of lino. lam-
inex table. 'Flour', 'Sugar'. clock
hands crawling. sliding door. sleepout.
venetians. naphthalene balls. back door.
flywire slap. tea leaves behind camellias.
sun through pickets. freshly mown couch.

more than half a sonnet

round the corner beside a lamp post an open empty
black suitcase waiting for a starfish flung on a beach

facing east and an apricot pip rubbed from truth to hurt
to boat and the unresolved yearning between falling seventh

and rising third and a kite in search of sky and the
unlonely 'aarrk' of a raven and all our suburb's

show bags of dreams and forgets and the weight of this
suitcase? weight of silence? weight of smoke? weight of why?

Nannup Diary

do you see the river as spittle?
silence, staves unplayed,
bracken it's own language

tuarts in their ragged tweeds,
small birds plucking.
see the river as spittle?

leaves shushing their names,
light gone sepia, hinting at moisture,
bracken's lyrics in slang

car roars across what was.
thinking with bark?
settles, yes, the river

these unwet days, hankering
for rain, sky closing,
bracken sounding betweens

necessity here, sanctity,
where ends the understory?
bracken's the hours unheard.
river sits, rippled

Kulin

it's Saturday, saloon. it's coins
stacked on bar towel and ponies of

beer. it's race seven from Doomben
and the jangle of a pinny

and banter between the boys.
it's the flywire slap. it's talk of

rain. it's Clarrie with three teeth
in beanie. it's frayed carpet and

Chef's Special on blackboard. it's the
whirr of fan. it's wheat yields and 'your

round' and 'yeah, school's closing'. it's
salt and vinegared and stale. it's

the head price for ewes and pressed tin
silence. its saloon, Saturday

hieroglyphics of now?

people,
there's a wide sky and untrammelled footpath out here
while you're in there on small stools crocheting stories.
people

used to
trim the bottoms off flowers, change the water, re-
arrange the stems to conjure randomness/order.
used to.

could you?
pull yourself back, smudge under and shimmy into
the scribbles of cirrus, hieroglyphics of now?
could you

stay close to the thrum of us, bang it on your knee,
bleed true?

(every colour makes yellow)

rarely shining – not for crows
no, the envelopes are more
while to drive up into dawn
before rain, the air tinctured
stolen from the lane of own
lifting lid, piano teeth
may take sides in homes of rest
RO G BIV isn't complete
but jaundiced were the streetlights
thunks, yes, the hue for that past
who sailed the seas, submarine
just that, the re-membering
then mustard and sepiaed
but amber wasn't the sun

enough notes for disappointment

blue by the net of impossible dreams
just because you're happy
it's getting loud in the silence
if I could have kept things just like that
sixteen years wide
earliest datable memory?
the river is late
as though hinting at shyness
we may lose this and that
on the pad I carried that day
would have used 'shapling' for 'foetus'
all blue on blue
but striding back towards the light

contrapunctus a 4

becoming
becoming unglued, seeking other gravities   seeing
    becoming unglued, seeking other gravities

unglued, seeking other gravities   seeing the black inside-
the black in the blue   the weight of tomorrow?
   becoming unglued, seeking other gravities   seeing
        seeing the black in the blue   the

outness   the weight of tomorrow?   dead
  becoming unglued   lying so beautifully, seeking other
the black inside-outness   lying
weight of tomorrow?   dead bird, one wing point-

bird, one wing pointing skyward   night, singing
dead birds   the inside-outness, mirrors
so beautifully, seeking other dead birds
ing skyward   night, singing the lines of hands

the lines of hands   losing north   as if there'll be
into night   losing
    night, singing the lines of hands
      as if there'll be forgetting

some sad fact about tomorrow   sky-
north, wings   singing the lines of forgetting,
    singing the lines of forgetting
  skyward, pointing   losing north, wings

ward
point-
losing wings
     flight, or more the idea of it
              the lines

ing   hearing some sad fact about gravities
  singing the lines   the inside-
out-
     about gravities   skyward,
of forgetting   seeing the black

   lying so beautifully under the hand
ness   being some sad fact
pointing under   the inside-outness, mirrors
inside-outness   lying

  the inside-outness   as if there'll be
about gravities   becoming unglued, mirrors
into night some sad fault   becoming
so beautifully under the hand as if there'll be some

some sad fault about tomorrow   being some sad
into the blue losing wings singing the lines of
unglued seeking other blues   seeing
sad fault about tomorrow   lying so beautifully,

fact about gravities   the weight of solitude?
forgetting, losing north the weight of solitude?
the black inside-outness the weight of solitude?
seeking other dead birds the weight of solitude?

all the thoughts

concerned for smallers –
all the drowning bees

late afternoon blood,
sun on the eyelids

where sits the god of
mauve and in-betweens?

but smudge and swarm and
smear sound like they feel

if all the thoughts were
to flock and seek north

while the diamet-
er of solitude?

and if was as full
a sentence as why?

a kind of swimming

can hear the black in the blue   looking up
                                 you took the fit in water,
    all your déjà vus in a dance   rubbing
fingers across bottle-top sky, just you, at the angle
        of nought   sucking
spangles of r.e.m.   at the tilt

of whim and wind   tilt-
ed, spinning, cirrus speaking   up
      words   the lanes sucking
their own   lunar pull on water
                   for some hard while, at the angle
of singing   rubbing

at glass and wonder and nigh   rubber-
ised, a writhe of unthought   tilt-
     ed, green to pink to blue   and angu-
lar, working the geometry of cloud   up,
        smell of theft and metal, morning, water,
       song of birds   sucking,

no north to intuit, nil magnetics   sucking
         remembereds   rubbing
nil   a ripple, self-contained, water
seeking other shores   tilt-
ed, spooned for stopping   up,
licking sky   so easy to make an A angle

```
into an I, horizontal insistence              angu-
         lar, ornamental                      sucking,
   a kind of swimming, a stroke, only arms not up,
more electric than muscular               rubbing,
       eight parts light, thirteen parts dark, tilt
of golden mean beyond you                 water,

waiting                          in the absence of water-
marks and tide, not flotsam               angle
of leaving                       as if felled, tilt-
ed, thrill of you in bark                 sucking
existence                                 rubbing
    meniscus, remaindered        cradled in up,

moored, rolling      left us         sucking
     at tongue and air               and rubbing
at now           inflected       yes, looking up
```

equal lengths

soothed and aching. until then. make the music they should.
yes, heard it fall. though blinkered. obeying the rules of
too few. by the tin foil sea. islands dolloped out there.

luminescent. three, out there. stunted tongues. looking in.
washing, licking. steeped walls. and were you taken, taken
under? smudged. or tossed, flotsam? the lighthouse. were you

expecting to be found? facing all ways and not. messaged,
bottled. exclamation mark. alongside the pike fish.
on a sentence too long for breath. conch shell. for sense.

tangle of rope. though from here. on squeaky sand. uncorked
and brittle. distance across braille of salt and tide? on
a skerrick of message paper. measures something like.

phone number, date. hypotenuse. and a plea. for the squared
sides. request. of h. in a faltering ball point.
h squared. (name, address). hope. for contact. equal lengths
of hope

Masks

the soup of us

quite like it.
the soup of
us. flywire
slap. banter.
dog whines. 'Spooks',
again. soup.
napping. tilt
of sleep/wake.
coughs. Nick Cave
gravelling.
the soup. chat.
kettle thrums.
like it. laugh-
ter. of us

unclearing

open to the wind, not
sheltered, not screened. open,
believing. open to

silents. open to think-
ing, no compass, no north.

and open to whys. op-

en to beyonds. open
to tide and waxing gib-
bous moon. open to in-

sidious burrs of doubt.

open to chafing. op-
en to because. open
to blister. open, un-

clearing. open to knot

Thurs

bottle top on concrete. piss-
ing twice against lemon tree.

skin of plum. hum of fish tank
water filter. when you get

there, tell me. this crooked life.
the Dean Martin cold shower.

are you, are you well? clench of
gum trees. a more willing aud-

ience. the hour of moving
metal. invented sweetness.

hope scrapes gravel. talked before
about stories. so many

words for sister. the lights fin-
ally close. and further? day

these bleak days

these are bleak days
bleak days are these
are these bleak days?
days, these are bleak

bleak are these days
days bleak are these
are these   days?
bleak   are these

     these are bleak
bleak   these days
days   are bleak
   these bleak days

bleak   these
bleak days
        these

              are days
               bleak

the stolen one

won't be as good as the stolen one,
so no, you don't write it.
I write it

but it's a sullen, bruised sky tonight.
petulance? a form of
engraving?

then you, not me, with your coloured bones
of forget. spelling of
'cuisinaire'?

lines empty, cursive immaculate.
an unrhymer has moved
in the storm

then this algebra of yearning,
my voice, you singing

the hush

it's just that, yeah, the hush, the trigonometry
of because, but, no, not always logic but yeah,
art hankers for it's hit of white and, yeah,
course, just sluice away, do your forgetting
in private 'cos no, this is a wide road for
thin thinks and, yeah(!), should've done the leaving
of blues to greens to reds, the yoga breathing,

but no, there is no polite retreat here – the
traffic of fraud is in flow and yeah,
absolutely, s'all done with ramps and cuisinaire
rods and rote learning and you, yes you with
your good ears and air traffic controlled angst,
no, you can't buy the hiss of liquid nitrogen on
skin, can't buy it, nah, can't buy the hush

thanxxs for contributing

and i was soaring along,
halfway through,
i love how you can go that way

began to fall in love with it,
towards the end
and soaring along

found curious,
what's going on?
sorry, i love how you can go that way tho

began to collapse on me,
seems to fall over itself
while i was soaring along

don't get where it's going,
music of it not the strongest,
sorry, i love how you can go that way tho

left me puzzled,
doesn't give me enough, sorry,
i love how you can go that way tho –
i was so soaring along

is it?

the incessant readying for rain?
phonetics of a fecund tongue?
all that letting?
leaves unmoved?
the impending morrow?
secular?
the sound of furniture?
honourable?
nicer (never use nice) in heat?
preferable?
the scent of a damp flannel?
sacred?
the needles?
me?

the purpling

out, running to stand still,
waiting for Venus – first up,

letting the purpling do its work,
sunshine seeping into pillow,

dreams translating the warmth,
slinking down, eyes along

the surface, drowning in cuts of
blue and silver and sunshine,

bled of urgents, the purpling,
keeping the words from the damp,

brittle as kindling, stacked
neat and ready 'neath the

galvanised tin of hope,
doing the work, licking silence,

drowning in horizon and
soft focus, rolling meaning in

the absence of a tongue,
the purpling, left-hand fingers

up and down the neck, mantra
of memory, right hand

drawing out breves for now,
letting, cool torso of

Salmon Gum, holding this tree,
brailling its oneness, its purpling,

in the park, rusted songs of swings
just vacated, memories

of play and flight, letting
the purpling do its work

the point?

1 infinity (1)

the point. point is. point one. pi. three
point. then it's bridal train of num-
bers to infinity. as a
kid went looking. needed to find
infinity. find it in the
home. touch it. scratched a hole in the
back of a doll's mirror. held it
to another mirror. peered through
the hole. infinity. found it.
a hallway to infinity.
had it. kept on coming back to
the mirror. the point? three point. pi's
infinity. a kid. found it

2 trees

been talking to trees. out. out and talk-
ing. with the shabby tuarts. their burnt
torsos, discoloured leaves. been talking
about the remembered. been talking
about rings. about what's in us and
what's skin. about diameters. a-
bout circumferences. the radii
of trees. they liked that. a kind of truth
to their spurtings. something measura-
ble. to be written down. remembered.
liked it. radii. sounds woody as
well. maths and wood. they asked me about
my rings, my width, my radii. I
said it was depth. I saw it as depth.
a plumb-line. line to a well. said I'd
given up on radii and di-
ameters. no pi. no maths. we stopped
there. at width. at depth. the point? why
does there always have to be a point?

3 blood

it's not blood but sap. viscous, sticky. that's what they told
me. a sugary ground-seeking ooze. blood's more metal-
lic in scent, more fluid. they said that. yours is thick in
the veins, thick, and in those cold limbs of yours, almost stat-
ic. dried and it becomes a stained glass they said. they said
that. like windows in church. a well muscled Jesus on
the cross. as a kid I'd stare at that window, entranced,
horrified, stare then look away. at the pew in front,
the rib-caged ceiling. all those smooth and bevelled edges
of wood. wood and sap. in our backyard the fat-headed
ants like rope up the torso of tree, engorging sap.
blood and sap. at me. and tomorrow they'll come again

4 the room

the room was red, yes, more red than I remembered.
seats in half a hexagon. I got in early
on the day and rehearsed. recital was at five.
five's not my favourite number. red's not my col-
our, never liked red. why are concert halls red? I
had the glock near the front of the stage. lights were be-
hind me. that was it. the light and shadows. that and
the rope ladder. I called it that. the bit in the
piece. hardest mallet work. the rope ladder. had to
get across that. only that and the shadows. my
head took out half a page. the page with the rope lad-
der bit. gone to me. numbed out. that's what undid me

5 silence

used to hunger for silence in a
piece. silence and stopping. fat bricks on
the stave. used to. then silence took me.
slice lives inside silence. silence un-
folded me. undid me. I live in-
side silence. sliced me. lives inside. tac-
et used to be my favourite word

6 as a kid

as a kid. counted cowboys in the
bricks. in the sleepout. night. milky flour-
escent through the sliding door window.
and the mopoke. minor third of mo-
poke. through the louvres. wooden tones of
mopoke. minor third. like a glock. two
notes on a glock. wooden. as a kid.
louvres. slivering the mopoke's call

infinity (2)

had a friend called infini-
ty. let me down. failed me. should
have known. slippery sideways
eight. rope preset for hanging.
led me to the hallway. to
the red room. kicked the timber
from beneath me. turned out the
lights. cut the ladder. left me.
should never have looked. the point?
does there have to be a point?

the one of us

one is the fret and first on top of zero and
morning is what we drew with the sun in the corner,
at our desks, all urgent, tongues awry and
the fact that ants like fingernails was the
beginning of a beautiful clasp of hours but beauty's
of little consequence measured against the
summer of all our contentments, for

summer with its flywire slack and stretch, days
of shimmering bitumen and brindled leaves, the
beginning of the bake and rise of us,
the ache and yearn and drip but just
at that moment it was the house, the windows, the clouds,
morning in crayons, our Christian names, only the
one of us, pencilled proud on the back

the hours

the hour, hours fall, fall slow, slowly, leaves
tick, tick quiet, quietly, my leashed, leashed mind,
mind ticks, ticks and, and falls, falls quick, quickly

sky bleeds, bleeds in, in one, wonder, drunk
cloud, clouding, clouding a, around, 'round now, now's
my, my sea, season, season of, of then

a crow, crow thieves, thieves sigh, silence, lent
things, things dig, dig his, history, even, ev-
en here, here I lick, lick day, déjà vu

truth is, isn't, fully, fully in,
interlocking, fingers, fingers and, and my,
my pickets, pickets thrum, thrum with, with news

wind combs, combs the, no, disturbs where, where
does, does air, air stop and skin, skin be, skin begin?

the groove of you

on the footpath you're all ant,
much looking down,
cutting against the groove of you

and yes, you feel better empty,
like a line not working,
an ant, black-roping thought

in the house you grew up in,
propped, defying the gibbous,
cutting against the groove of you

a cloud breathes you in
and out into bark and path,
ant blind, antennae touching

'let's do it by room' you say,
even your torso accepting,
half-cut, in that groove of you

but in this alluvial silence
it's your walk, not mine,
all ant, blind, searching for sweetness,
cutting through the groove of you

the colour of healing

it's a thick silence,
unrehearsed and accidental,
with the house suddenly empty.
rare, in a home like this –
grand piano, two cellos, violin, guitar –
three musicians and a dog,
Bach chaconnes, Chopin preludes and
high pitched whines joining cello duets

has me thinking though,
about the repositories of silence
because it's been here and waiting,
in the 45 degrees of stairwell, the angle
providing harbour, a balloon of silence
the colour of healing

the boys

the boys, circled, in jeans, shirts
untucked, beers and banter,

loosening, back slapping, real
estate prices, golf tales, the

boys, who's round? unbuttoning,
stubbies and schooners, un-

finishing, Wednesday after-
nooning, the boys, in this

pranged up moment of shared
and shed untruths and

bruises, the boys, beering,
untangling, cruising, jaunty

and blooming, the boys, in the
ambered half-light, the boys

out here

out here, a different
quality of silence, as if
sifted, as if wrung of

possibility, as
if notes, the missing fourth and sev-
enth from a pentaton-

ic scale. out here no dis-
sonance, out here where the fur of
thought won't crackle static,

out here just a petha-
dined blue. here you let, here you pause
and permit then pour, here

you lick behind shadows, find flight,
propose theories for déjà vu

napkin man

(1) a.m.

aren't the way you should be – light just
leaking, neaped, thoughts snared on
the brown paragraph of jetty.

night has picked you clean – pike fish,
flung, one eye away from weed,
just light and not the way you should be.

angst has loosened nails,
sweat left its measure on the
brown jarrah graph of pity

and the knowns? conch is curled
search for song, before rain sepiaed
light, you, not the way you should be.

flotsam's a salt tossed scheme
while you're all eyelids and unclocked
on this brown jetty of paragraph

and the rolls of surf? rocking horse
manes of a child in wake
on a brown paragraph of jetty?
light, you, not the way you should be

(2) p.m.

no, you don't believe in crows
nor in the bright or buttoned or thieved,
but something in those three lost 'arrks'

has you back and paddocked,
easterlies singing through the wires
though no, you never believed in crows,

more in Spitfires and verandas
and angles of battle,
lost in the wee art of humming

leaving you today, in shimmer heat,
reading childhood scrawl of cirrus,
tilting t'wards belief in crows

but the seconds dwarf, gut strings
and Bach recoil on ebony,
something in those last three darks

provides the sustenance of shadow,
pulls you from glare to gliss,
same thing in those lost three 'arrks'
that has you not believing in crows

(3) _.m.

yes, you pull dross from pockets,
place it in a bin not yours –
a napkin man, of course,

one from each of the four,
those crumpled clouds of moment,
now dross pulled from pockets,

into laneway, but halted –
cat? rodent? ripple of unthink?
being, of course, a panic man

while the moon, toenail clipping
that it is, gifts you with
possibility of docket,

then, nearing home, lust kindling,
night entwined by silk and kiss
'cos you're a man of lick not plan,

at door, fumbling for keys/dreams
and while one fits, t'others fold
for you are, of course, a napkin man,
pulling dross from pockets

me?

but yes, breathing in ants,
all the legs, the sixes

of rhyme. these are thin days –
the 'we' in 'between' has

been extracted. and when
I shit in the rain grate

I hear rats come running.
the oarsmen of thought stroke

across the neap slack face
of us. have this dream of

being eclipsed by the
moon of Nullus. but then

oblivion has four
syllables too many

lingers

it's a dangerous light near the surface. is-
lands. drawn out silence. and like sails in my hands.
these habits. frail spring afternoon. does not meet
my eyes. gnarled. netted with shadows. a mess of
ripples. the ebb, forecast of loss. using my
own words. hands twitching the jetsam. verticals
surrendered to smart haze. a meniscus of
thought. perfect trajectory. but losing north.
the Sound remembers. the mouth is the eyes. cut
the sea from the beach. squinting against. lingers.
stumps of jetty, reminders. fat matchsticks. flot-
sam of seens. neap. scent of dried weed. gap between
sensation and sense. haphazard paint strokes. then
shirrs. near the skin surface, like doubt. dangerous

east block

seductive, velour to
tongue, that gush and gurgle
and throaty song, that lounge
of mouth that says sip, breathe,
take it slow, long. where are
you now, my petite friend,
my verdant hall runner

of welcome, my mae-
stoso of imbibe and
wonder? why, you are there,
beside at table, beck-
oning dive, swim, lift this
fathomless goblet to
lips, let's toast to Mangen!

display pome

ritual is no self-
medication (entry).
shagpile silence (lounge). your
songs of other (master-
bedroom). serrations and
tines (dining). mother
(family) hides moth
and other. (kitchen) when

did gravy become
jus? (studio) ears
don't have lids. (bathroom)
scent of week-old wet flannel.
(laundry) bop and muck
it. (veranda) sipping sky

darks

Chopin saw Bb minor as charcoal
in ICU its your name and the date
number of truths equals number of cuts
ravens prefer to roost on dead branches
ill's a good word – deals with it succinctly
congregation of tuarts, all standing
it's a dangerous light near the surface
not recuperating, always the next
cirrus smeared, hinting, smudging the language
venetians slivering the mopoke's call
the undead aren't writing books about it
raking the coals, making night in the grate
all purpled, flywired, Sunday afternooned
while in my shirt box mind, pinning moth words

chamber musing

(1) 43 days

all on foot, drug ripe and addled,
Tramadols and Endones puppeting mice

in the peripherals, trekking lanes and
limestone, withered grapes atop walls, to the West

sky smeared peach, on the demolition site
pink ribbons around the trunks of two tuarts –

heritage listed? termites? brake lights and
brittling couch grass, the bruising of a

week closed, sutures of hours – clockwise
is off. to the wharves, slap of ropes

and tide, 'Spliethoft', Dutch, engorging.
it's a Vaselined moon tonight, March brooding

(2) venn intersects

in this convalescence – good word that with its
gauze-like length and syllabic wrap – been

practicing the lost art of waiting, bus and
train stations, doctors' rooms, never enough

shade or new *New Ideas*, been watching,
the wizened and the upright, figs ripening,

footpaths that flow like prose then trip like
misspellings, been rubbing paperbark trees,

listening in on frogs, been mulling over the
difference between learned and remembered,

the venn intersects, making a mantra
of 'clockwise is off' while pondering the

origin of knowns, the mind that did
the choosing, hands that shape our days

(3) rope armies

taken my lungs to ocean, remembering
that on taps, clockwise is off, though

that is my truth, my tomorrow, not that
of the clock hands and been thinking

'bout tides and un-neaping, and lets call it
global swarming though we'll never get there

of course, when, for every ant there's
a human – they know that, 'cos for us

'mining' means 'mine' and we're more blind
than they are and while we're making

books for our faces they're forming rope
armies to bind and save the world

bent truth and belief

(i)

bent truth – call it that,
the horizon, the plot,
smudged with island,
smeared by jaundiced sunlight,
a join the dots of ships
and gulls hovering like thought.
along the scrim two fishermen
casting out and out,
hooked on chance,
the sudden jerk.
Tuesday, no sound track here,
only the wind
working in a blunt HB,
across and back,
on silence.
but these first spits of rain,
from whose story are these?

(ii)

too many birds, yes,
too many for logic,
a squadron of black cockatoos,
cries like can openers,
sharp around the rim of sky.
collective leading,
a tag team of wakes.
too many for a chorus of updrafts,
too many for the thoughts
of too few,
too many for the sullen work of bridges.
winged fiction, air-pocketed,
scythed from page,
sleek and paragraphed.
too many for lighthouses,
for regret,
too many for ships or why.
Thursday, etched on blue,
residue of clouds.
these birds, sly bells,
too many for an abacus,
for creeds or commandment,
enough for belief

and leave

leave bowls of water for the moon,
take the river's truth and gift it,
see all sides of wet things,
catch the rain and wind in separate hands

leave bowls of wind for the hands,
catch the moon's truth and wet it,
see all gifts in rain things,
take the river and water to separate sides

weave water and moon,
slake the river of gifts,
seed the truth with rain,
shake the river of separate lands

sleeve the moon,
wake the river,
sift rain,
hatch and leave

Moths

the line that failed me

almost like a flight of love,
how it thistles the lips,
all wings and anarchy

the attraction far beyond me
so jazz it up a bit more!
almost like a flight of love

I'm in it purely for its full outsourcing,
how it rim-shots around the mouth,
all wings and anarchy

spacing falls away too quickly
but that's the nature of an easement,
almost like a flight of love

as I resist the journey,
it's spiccato on the tongue,
wings and anarchy

but hey, I think it's linear,
a bit too incumbent,
just wings and anarchy,
almost like a flight of love

punctuated sky

the footpaths are sentences
five and half years of this
embrace the meaning of dry
an all too impatient clock
didn't do any leaving
I could sell you this moment
always the next, propped, bedded
meteorological
words asleep in their own skin
beyond the hush of syringe
but I'm running to stand still
shirt box mind, pinning moth words
and the unnecessary?
lost in punctuated sky

louvred light

it rises in scent and wet bracken
it doesn't need a wall around it
it's empty, further away than death
it could be dust motes, the soft focus
it's withered to nought but still singing
it pulls away, slides into regret
it's becoming unnecessary
it's written in the scrawl of cirrus
it whispers that north's not important
it's perforated and unbreathing
it's better in the absence of thought
it leaves moth-wing stains on forefingers
it's in the split lino, louvred light
it's yesterday, but no one's noticed

learnts

number of sips equals number of tastes
cirrus is a smeared, silent language
smother hides mother holds other
more salve in horizons than creeds
thinks spin but a moon librates
we're ants in the blind search for sweetness
monks can tell one silence from another
in ICU it's the day and your name
it's in forgetting, losing north
not long after I'm dead, you'll be dead
a peppermint brailles in bark
we're all wide-eyed in the sudden light
a hammer feels the purpose of a nail
and can see the black in the blue

in my absence

see the church? the people?
that congregation,
the crop of believers.
ants are like that –
have to march as one,
in time with others creeds.
variety, dichotomy,
dead thinkings – these
instincts aren't here, aren't
mine for the altar.
four hours, the pew biting me,
weak at my prayer-cushioned knees.
absolutes come dressed as hymns,
sense won't stain the humble

hopes

hope isn't blue or loose or lost.
hope is full.
hope isn't tearful or funny
or berserk.
hope is cumulus and shagpile.
hope isn't
mood or diameter or pinned.
hope is hinge

hope is note
and bottle and flotsam and found.
hope isn't
pulpit or coal-fired or concave.
hope is spinifex and singing.
hope is rain

still as moss

symphony of spits and drips,
scent of wet bracken,
so very still, still as moss

hills, like boxes underneath the green rug,
congregation of tuarts standing,
a symphony of spits and drips

time isn't vertical, isn't horizontal,
after rain, one syllable talk,
and so very very still, like moss

then looking up,
sky unmaking itself,
symphony of drips and spits

greys and khakis and verdant and glistening.
where sits the god of drizzle?
so very still, still as moss

and the bush is a church with its
naves and prayer cushions and incense,
a symphony of spits and drips,
so very still, still as moss

sonnet breathing

in for eight. the folded heat. North long
forgotten. all clean sheeted.
passepieding. for eight. the updraft
pressing. gusts of now. brush
strokes. sicilienning. tidal. in
for. soft as moth. deeper than
here. forty fathoms. in eight. stretched thrum-
ming. the shagpiled silence. in,

out. allemanded. dip and
push. two stringed guitar. but sighing, blown.
air trawled. call it the haar. lung's
flotsam. out for. sarabanded. pi-
ano accordioned. oth-
er music. gills of dawn. out for six

silence isn't yellow

silence isn't yellow, isn't cut-
lery. silence is a species of shag-

pile. silence is the venn circle, the
pond, next to the ocean of sound. silence

is a moth, looping and feeding on light
of now. silence is not a museum

not art gallery, each with their screaming
histories and hues. silence is spine on

feathers. silence is more horizontal than
vertical. silence is equal parts before and

after. silence tries to rhyme, then repeels itself.
silence is an only child. silence isn't

lonely. silence writes letters, doesn't send
them. silence is a shade of velour

moth words

number of sips equals number of
tastes. if you were
to lie like that, upside down. Chopin

saw Bb minor
as charcoal. cirrus is a smeared

silent language. legs propped against
wall, world. in ICU

its your name and the day.
smother hides mother holds other. if you were
to sit. raking

the coals, making night in the grate.
more salve in horizons

than creeds. lake gone to seed. ravens
prefer to roost on dead
branches. thinks spin but a moon

librates. eyes and mind in soft focus,
all elsewhere. ill's a good word –

deals with it succinctly. we're ants in
the blind search for sweetness.
if you were to

lose sight. congregations of tuarts,
all standing.

go with wind through
leaves and voices. it's a

dangerous light
near the surface. monks can tell one silence
from another. soles as creeds,

forgetting North. not recuperating, always
the next. not long after I'm dead

you'll be dead. if bark and clouds and
blood were text and thoughts
came in boats. number of

truths equals number
of cuts. a peppermint brailles in bark.

and if was as fuller sentence
as why. venetians slivering
the mopoke's call. we're all wide-eyed

in the sudden light. if you were to
pretend. the undead aren't

writing books about it. a hammer feels the
purpose of nail.
play,

let the hours be
plasticine. all purpled, flywired,

Sunday afternooned. can see the black
in blue. the shape of if? while

in my shirt box mind
pinning moth words

propped

in the dia-
ry of clean be-
ginnings. gift of
ponder? you make
an entry. plas-
tic beneath sheet.
listen to that
a line about
clouds. absent but
near? dialect
of cirrus. night
nurse moth. how
light goes sepi-
a before rain.
beyond index.
augmented fourth
remembering.
ache's interval
hovers. the smell
of wet earth. all
your yesterdays.
resolving in
songs of loose pick-
ets. heelless. how
the wind stole your
stories. slapping.
into unrhyme
sold them elsewhere.

cuff, swab. then lat-
er. memory's
pylons. much lat-
er. fluky veins.
resolving out
how you find your-
self. drips. stooped ov-
er. neap tide. lap
ping at these same
lines. feeding you.
to scree of now
from a vast un-
mapped. inland sea

a crooked eye

as I wash me in you
the clock fibs, night folds while
you hover, watch me in you

the light antique now,
lemoned at the edges
as I wash me in you

moths are drunken deckhands,
jigging, stopping only as
you hover, watch me in you

if you were to run fingers
but no, no maps, too soon
as I wash me in you

two notes from mopoke drip,
break the meniscus of thought
while you hover, watch me in you

and the moon casts a crooked eye
over the imagined
as I wash me in you,
as you hover, watch me in you

and the wind

the wind blew through us. we were small that
day, there and not. sea was scuffed, frothed, whipped,

smear of land far out where blue skirts blue.
wind blew through us. swept us clean, swept us

of tales and ache. we were lost that day,
found but not. one gull, high up, wheeled and

watched. blew through us. we were song that day,
free on the stave, note then note, spume and

a whiff and dried weed, lick and boom of
waves, nudge of groyne. the wind blew through. we

were sand that day, sand and salt and shell
and curled. we were grain that day. wind through

us. glint of sun off the quilt of brine.
we were small and hope. the wind through us

drinking why

I guess you can hear the worms working.
was your fall gracious?
you've one wing splayed, pointing skyward

your plumage suggests diurnal,
male obviously, being so garish
and I guess you can hear worms working

eyes open, glazed like stars forsaken,
piercing infinity, drinking why,
one wing splayed skyward

and ants will come, seething black ropes,
swarming, feeding on your story.
I guess you'll still hear the worms working?

then wind, whittling at hollow bones,
thieving your commas, your full stops,
one wing still splayed, skyward

'too close to the sun' they prattle,
but too far from dreams?
with one wing splayed skyward.
I guess you won't hear the worms working

Moons

the less heard

there are eight limbs sprouting from
the trunk of this tree,

one for each of the senses and one
for earth, moon and sun, so I'm

running fingers, inhaling, licking at,
watching this warm musty bark,

listening for the less heard,
the other side,

a rhyme with orange

Venus

Venus, my first friend,
is up waiting, watching.
what she sees, of course,

needs no window.
what she sees is us,
blue marble spilt
from pouch,

moth hole in black satin,
an idea,
yes, an idea

unknown skies

do the forgetting
backwards in now
breathe away

eye the plane to nought
float with dust motes
work the neck

serendipitise
look, unknown skies
rub three trees

knead a waning moon
walk the other
syncopate

and under the bed?
forgettings

two notes

you have this memory, aged 7 perhaps,
in the sleepout and tucked in, your brother

a breath away across the lino,
and you have the scene before, counting

cowboys in the bricks, Dad on the piano
with the hymns for the week, and you have

the lighting, kitchen fluoro milky through the
crinkled glass window atop the sliding door,

but most of all you have the moment –
two notes, minor third, descending,

the mopoke's call, random perhaps, or on the
minute? matters little, the wooden two notes

of mopoke, through the slivers of louvres,
clear as moon, as yesterday

the weight of angst?

leafless, nervous
feather or bark?
bracken's language
while losing north

gibbous thinkings
system of tree
lonely two notes
click of why's tongue

desiccated
moon paints in talc
holds Southern Cross
song of mopoke

thrumming forgets
now's syllabics
the weight of angst?
within it's limbs

the same moon

it is the same moon but if
you lick it you'll find that
it's not and when I was in
grade one I watched him, in
suit made of tin foil and spoons,
take a few steps and say that
he did it for all of us and in
church Mum says 'dear Lord, I
have sinned' but she has not sinned
and I asked the moon what it felt
like to be trod on and I asked
the moon why we tell fibs
and the same moon said 'hurt and
to feel cleansed' and I asked was it
the steps or fibs that hurt?

the night for knots

suburbia slunk down,
Monday's shoulders shrugging off
the seduction of oil –

must be the night for knots.
and in the footpath's story
a page missing.

can hear the box tree dying,
crickling out its name.
rubbing fingers across

a shagpile sky,
where sits the god of mauve
and in-betweens?

two notes from mopoke,
wooden, not lonely

the moon's reminder

prefer boat to ship – sounds rounder, safer –
ten of them, a scattering, at all angles,
paper boats, only paper is for stories

people in one boat, sea unfolding,
wind scuffing cheeks –
prefer boat to ship – sounds fatter, safer

caught betwixt and neaped and between,
at the whim of moon's tug,
a paper boat, only paper is for stories

letters and boats make journeys, while
the tide is the moon's reminder –
prefer boat to ship – sounds rounder, fatter

but flotsam needs to be found,
lifted, held in cupped palms,
a paper boat, only paper is for stories

so I'm building a jetty of words, line by
plank by line, out to these
paper boats, only paper is for stories –
prefer boat to ship, sounds rounder, safer

seven sutures

fiction comes last.
Friday tales too
far distant so
fold me elsewhere,

for not the ache of
fiefdom, no, not your
'friends' of nil, nor be-
forehand of contract.
five steps to a moon?

sixteen hours, the canary
sings. coal mine deaf, mute and numb,
slinks on. denim drug of choice,
stitched into dollars and un-
sense. hum, mumbles, Tupperware
sealed in fridge, off as promise.
seven sutures, no ooze, yet

old stones

you'll go on ahead.
you'll tie the laces on the
sky. you'll brill the moon.

I'll bring up the rear.
I'll find old stones filled with pock-
ets. I'll tear my thoughts.

the sound of black

I understand the meaning
of her silence but don't have
a word for it so I scour
night sky for a term for the
sound of black between stars
and moon and meteorites and
planets and us and come up
with 'evol' and write it
down and then show it to her and
she says 'is that the root of
evolve like before stuff
moves or morphs?' and I say
'no, it's love backwards' and she
stares at me and says nothing

last bits

moon tugs at the
wet in me. earth

lays claim to the
pelt of me. a

crow waits to thieve
the night from me.

the cross gives a
glow to the guilt

in me. time winks
at the angst in

me. and you? you're
there with shirt box

and pins for the
last bits of me

his walk, not mine

tonight we're out waltzing the lanes,
Benjamin and me, he with his snout

in everything, me with my head seeking moons.
we visit the chooks three backyards up,

huddled in their roost, we engorge on
fallen unripe mulberries and olives,

we do the day's history of each verge,
remembering, of course, that it's his walk

not mine – at corners, a tug on leash and we
head that way. it's quiet out, breeze shushing

at tomorrow. later, rifling through the newly
arrived journal for a short story, my eyes

seek out dialogue – I need the chat,
the banter, roll of a syllable or two

fiction is necessary

but, upside down in the dark,
all the lyrics have fallen

to the bottom of the box.
turned, back to the dark ocean,

the strange wet lap of the beach,
and, as I risk vertigo,

riding a warm updraft to
hover and glide with the gulls,

all strokes, no answers, fending
off clocks and chessboards and clouds,

intravenous hits of doubt.
it's a furred logic this, as

truth makes its slow osmosis.
but the trick? don't read for plot

but they say

they say dust stops gathering after a
time on the fibs and scribbled skies that get

swept under to rest alongside grey balls
of dead slaters and moon slivers of toe-

nail clippings and I had a friend whose three-
year-old kept chattering about the dead

bunny beneath the bed and she thought it
make-believe till catching a whiff of what

the second hand as uncaretaker did-
n't forget where dark and darkness lie side

by side and a scrunched up bus ticket and
off cuts of prayer compare journeys and there,

a bookmark that questioned fate's page but they
say, after a time, dust stops gathering

www.ingramcontent.com/pod-product-compliance
Lightning Source LLC
Chambersburg PA
CBHW070912080526
44589CB00013B/1266